Best Latin Songs

Arranged by Marcel Robinson

CONTENTS

ISBN 0-7935-9818-4

HAL•LEONARD®
CORPORATION
7777 W. BLUEMOUND RD. P.O. BOX 13819 MILWAUKEE, WI 53213

Visit Hal Leonard Online at
www.halleonard.com

Always in My Heart
(Siempre én Mi Corazón)

Music and Spanish Words by Ernesto Lecuona
English Words by Kim Gannon

1. You are al-ways in my (2.) heart, _____ e-ven though you're far a-

way. _____ I can hear the mu-sic of _____ the song of love I sang with

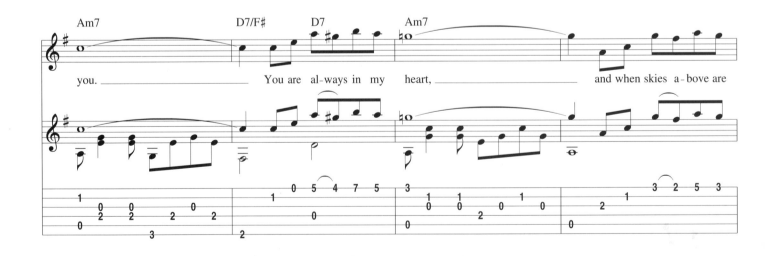

you. ____ You are al-ways in my heart, _____ and when skies a-bove are

Spanish Lyrics

Verse
Siempre esta én mi corazón
El recuerdo de tu amor,
Que al igual que tu canción
Quitó de mi ama su dolor.
Siempre esta én mi corazón
La nostalgia de tu ser
Ya hora puedo comprender
Qué dulce ha sido tu perdón.
La visión de mi soñar
Me hizo ver con emoción,
Que fue tu alma inspiración
Donde aplaqué mi sed de amar.
Hoy tan sólo es pero verte
Y ya nunca más perderte,
Mientras tanto que tu amor,
Siempre esta én mi corazón.

El Cumbanchero

Words and Music by Rafael Hernandez

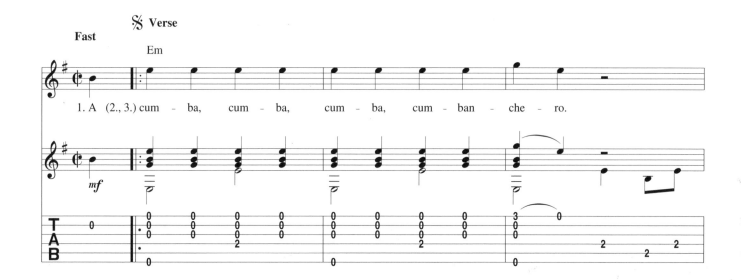

1. A (2., 3.) cum - ba, cum - ba, cum - ba, cum - ban - che - ro.

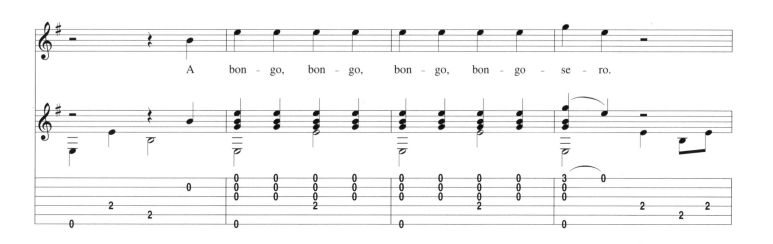

A bon - go, bon - go, bon - go, bon - go - se - ro.

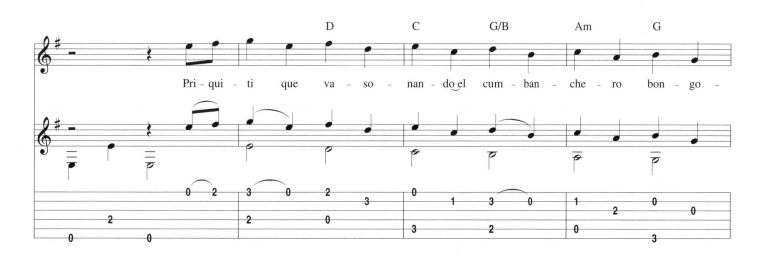

Pri - qui - ti que va so - nan - do el cum - ban - che - ro bon - go -

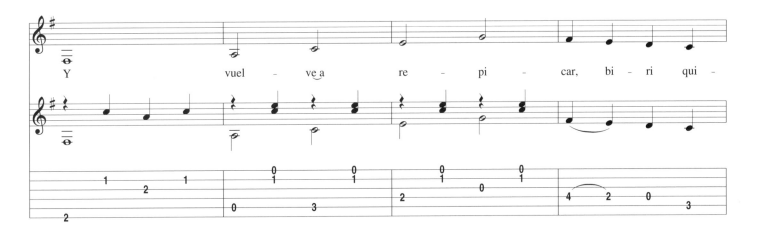

Y   vuel - ve a   re - pi - car, bi - ri qui -

D.S. al Coda

tí,   bum - bum - bá.   3. A

Coda

va.

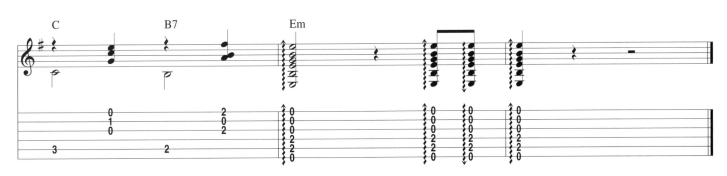

Bésame Mucho
(Kiss Me Much)

Music and Spanish Words by Consuelo Velazquez
English Words by Sunny Skylar

Drop D Tuning:

① = E ④ = D
② = B ⑤ = A
③ = G ⑥ = D

Intro
Moderately

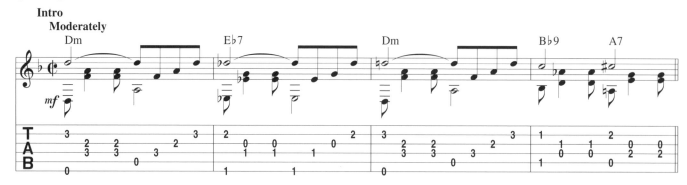

Verse

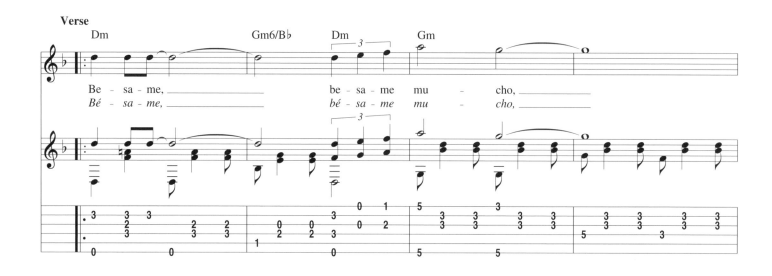

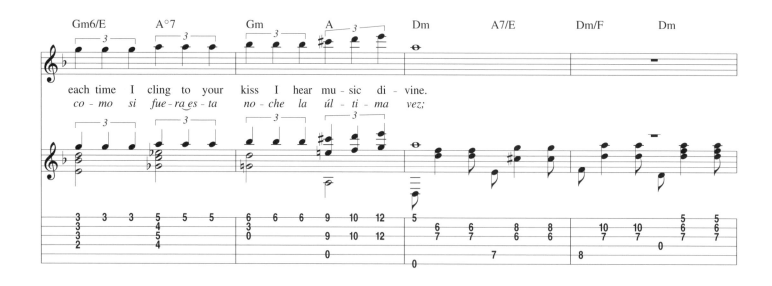

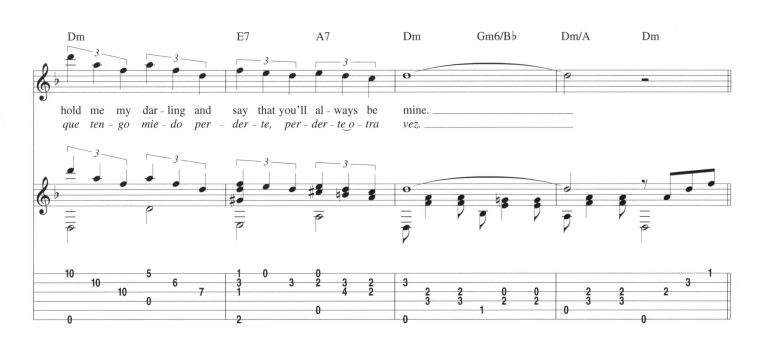

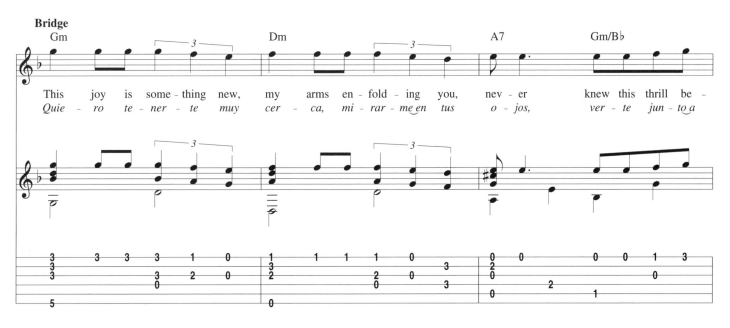

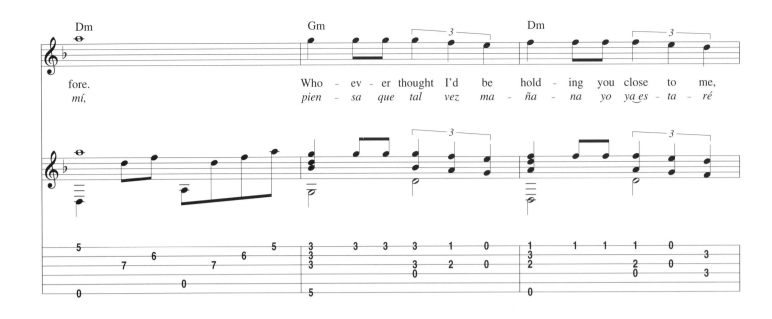

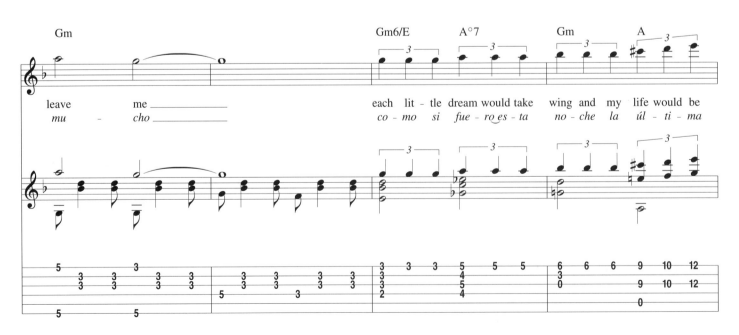

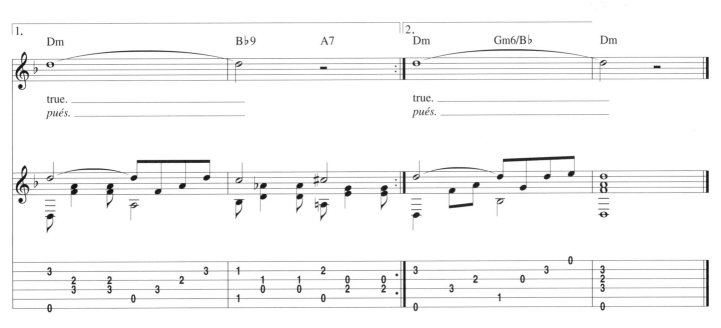

A Day in the Life of a Fool
(Manhá De Carnaval)

Words by Carl Sigman
Music by Luiz Bonfa

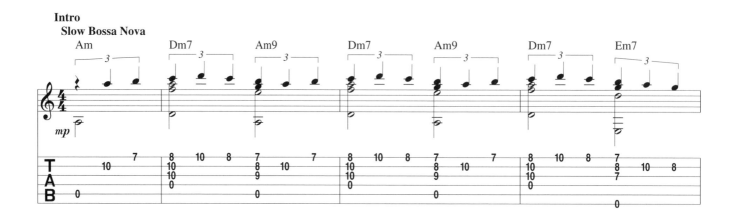

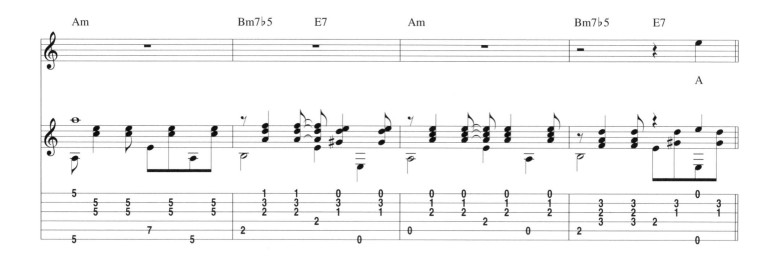

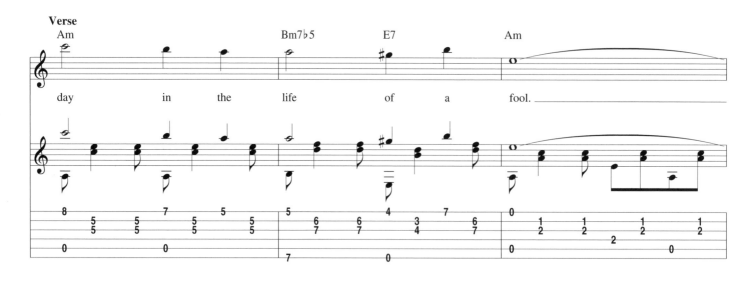

Frenesí

Words and Music by Alberto Dominguez

Drop D Tuning:
①= E ④= D
②= B ⑤= A
③= G ⑥= D

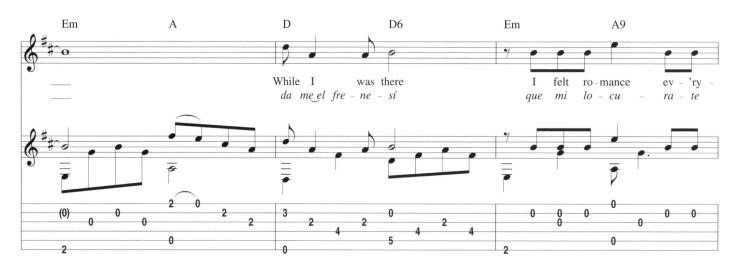

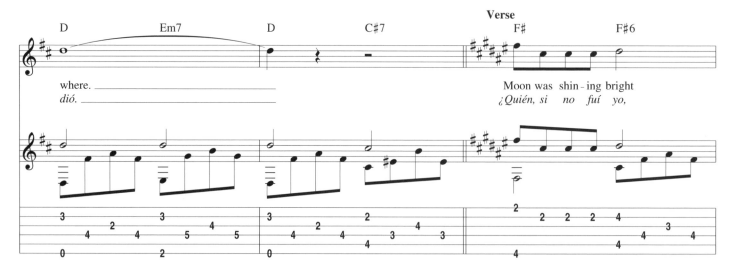

G#m7 C#9 F# F#6 G#m C#9
and I could hear laugh-ing voi-ces in the night:
pu-do en-se-ñar-te el ca-mi-no del a-mor,
F# F#6 G#m7 C#9 F# A7
Ev-'ry-one was gay, this was the start of their hol-i-day.
muer-ta mi al-ti-vez, cuan-do mi ar-gu-llo ro-dó a tus pies?
Chorus
Em7 A7 Em7 A7
It was fi-es-ta down in Mex-i-co, and so I stopped a while to
Quie-ro que vi-vas só-lo pa-ra mí y que tú va-yas por don-
Em7 A7 Em7 A7 D6 Dmaj7
see the show. I knew that fre-ne-sí meant please love me,
de yo voy, pa-ra que mi al-ma sea no-más de ti,

her lips just plead-ed   to   be   kissed.   Her eyes were soft as can-dle-
al - ma, pie - dad,   co - ra - zón;   *di - me que sa - bes tu sen-*

shine,   so how was   I   to   re - sist? _____
tir,   *lo mis - mo que sien - to   yo.* _____

_____ And now with-out   a   heart to   call   my   own, _____   a great - er   hap - pi - ness I've
_____ *Quie - ro que vi - vas só - lo   pa   -   ra   mí* _____   *y   que tú va - yas por don-*

The Gift!
(Recado Bossa Nova)

Music by Djalma Ferreira
Original Lyric by Luiz Antonio
English Lyric by Paul Francis Webster

di - ga que-eu meen - con ___ tro ne sse es ta - do. 3. Vo - ce

ce. ___ Do seu des - ti no vo - ce seu

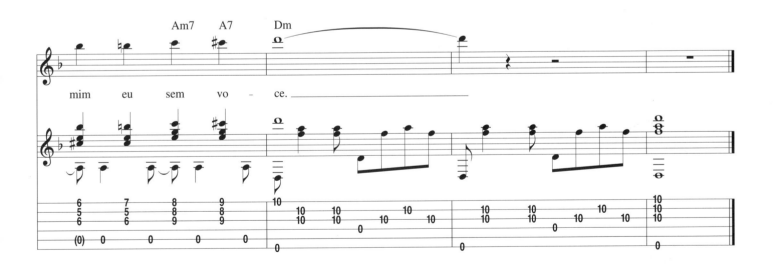

mim eu sem vo - ce.

Additional Lyrics

2., 3. Voce dei xou semquerer die xou
Uma sauda dee nor meen sue lugar
De pois no's dois cada qual a mer ce
Do sue desti no voce seu mim eu sem voce.

The Girl from Ipanema
(Garôta de Ipanema)

English Words by Norman Gimbel
Original Words by Vinicius de Moraes
Music by Antonio Carlos Jobim

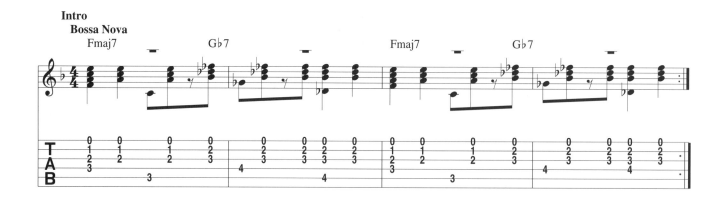

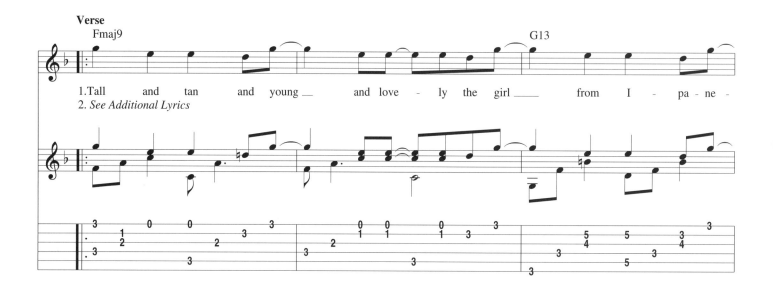

1.Tall and tan and young ___ and love - ly the girl ___ from I - pa - ne -

2. *See Additional Lyrics*

- ma goes walk - ing and when ___ she pas - ses, each one ___ she pas - ses goes,

Yes, _____ I would give my heart glad - ly _____ but each day

___ as she walks ___ to the sea, ___ she looks ___ straight a - head ___ not at me. ___

Verse

3.Tall and tan and young ___ and love - ly the Girl ___

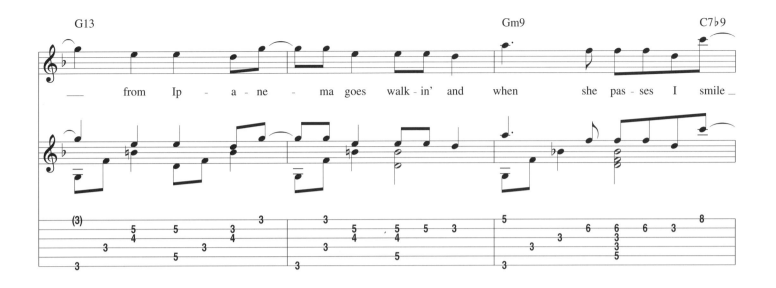

from Ip - a - ne - - ma goes walk - in' and when she pas - ses I smile __

but she does-n't see __ she just does-n't see

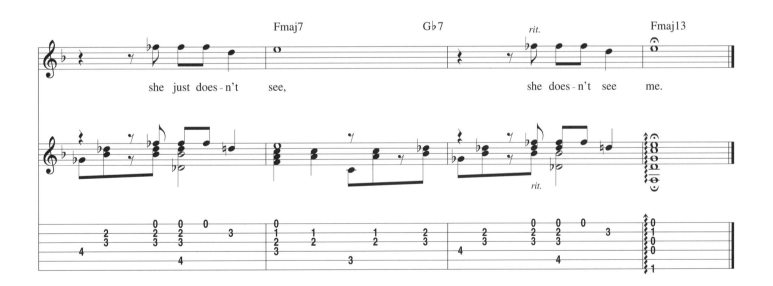

she just does-n't see, she does-n't see me.

Additional Lyrics

2. When she walks it's like a samba
   That swings so smoothe and swags so gentle that
   When she passes, each one she passes goes, "Ahh."

27

Granada

Spanish Words and Music by Agustin Lara
English Words by Dorothy Dodd

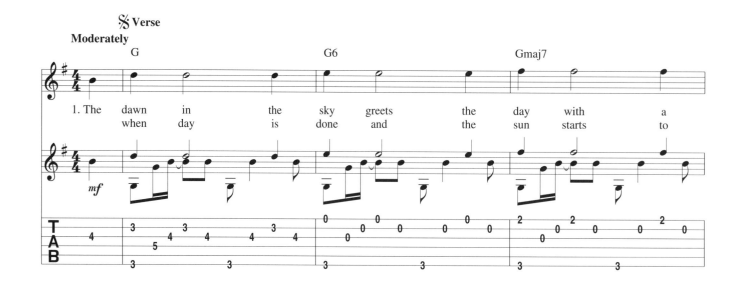

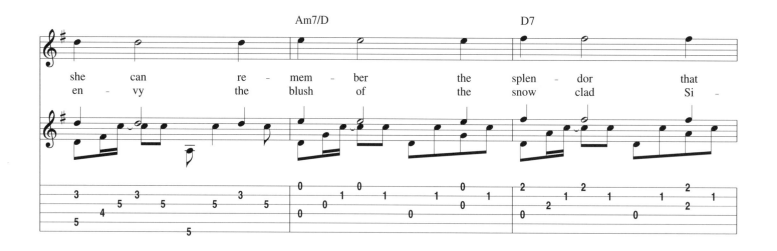

To Coda ⊕

Am7/D　　　　　　　　G

once was Gra - na - da. _____ It
er - ra Ne - va - da. _____

Bridge
G　　　　　　　　　　　　G6　　　　　　　Gmaj7

still can be found in the hills all a -

G　　　　　　　　　　　　Bm

round as I wan - der a - long, _____ en -

F#　　　　　　　　　　　　　　　　　Bm

tranced by the beau - ty be - fore me, en -

How Insensitive
(Insensatez)

Original Words by Vinicius de Moraes
English Words by Norman Gimbel
Music by Antonio Carlos Jobim

MCA Music Publishing

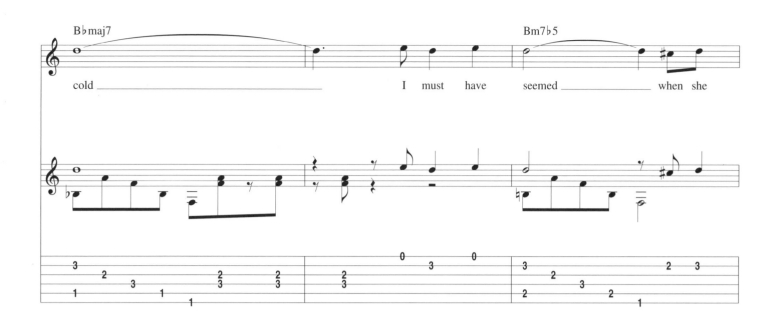

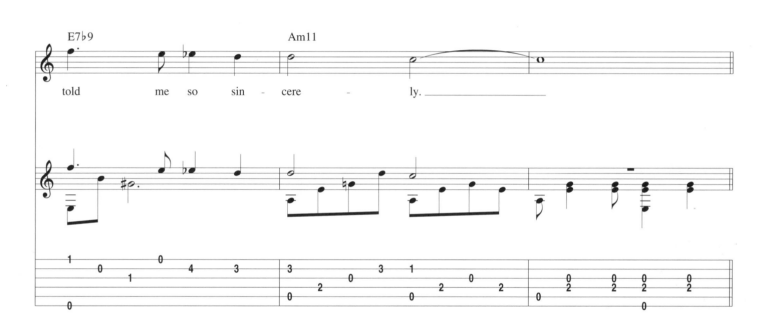

Chorus

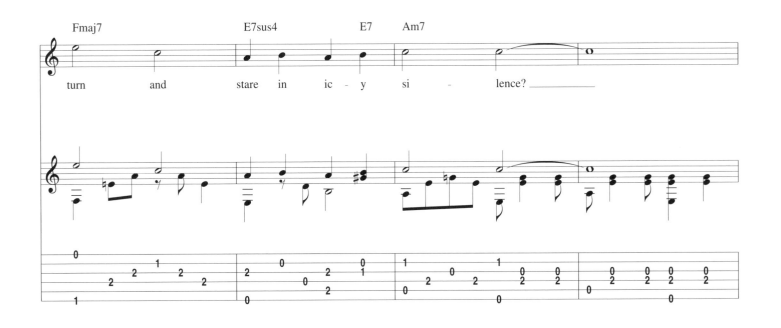

Inolvidable

Words and Music by Julio Gutierrez

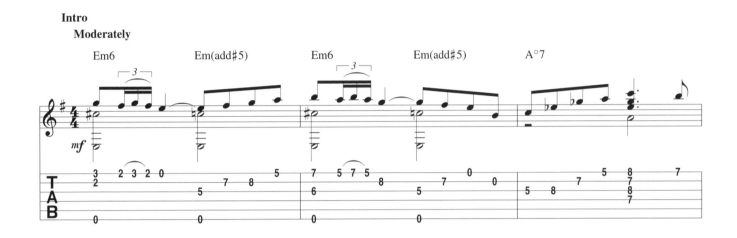

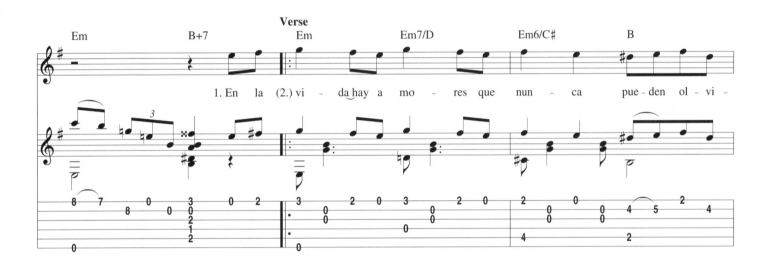

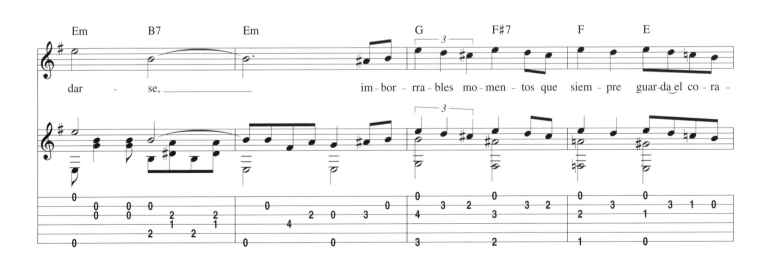

It's Impossible
(Somos Novios)

English Lyric by Sid Wayne
Spanish Words and Music by Armando Manzanero

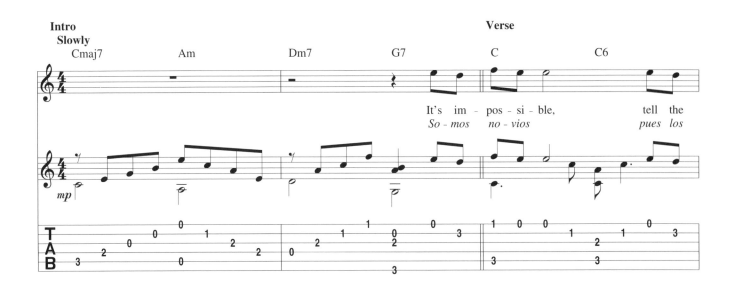

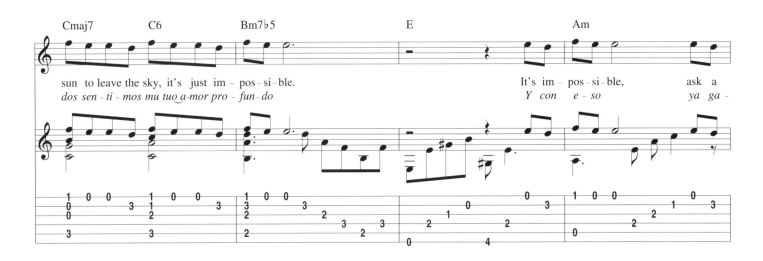

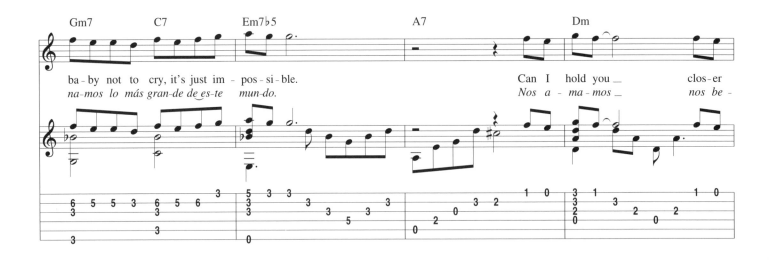

Malagueña

from the Spanish Suite ANDALUCIA

Music and Spanish Lyric by Ernesto Lecuona
English Lyric by Marian Banks

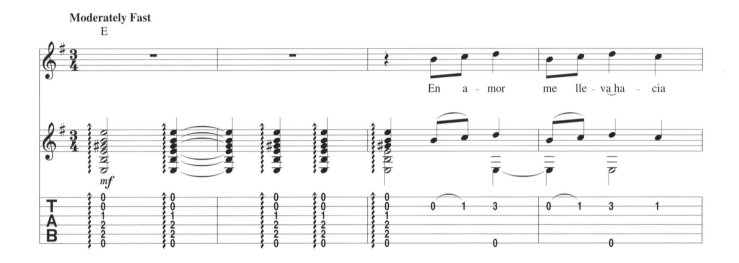

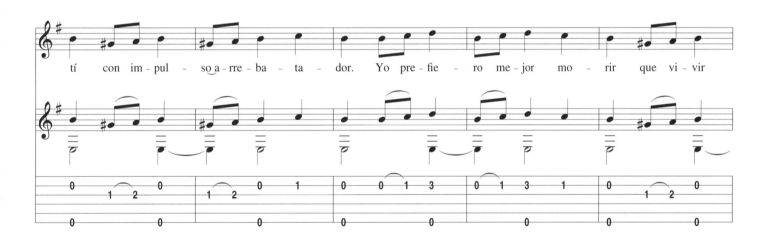

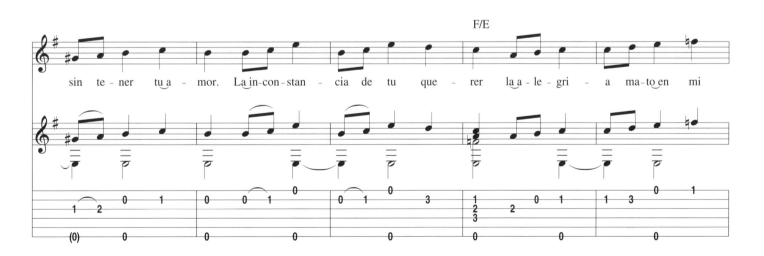

Perfidia

Words and Music by Alberto Dominguez

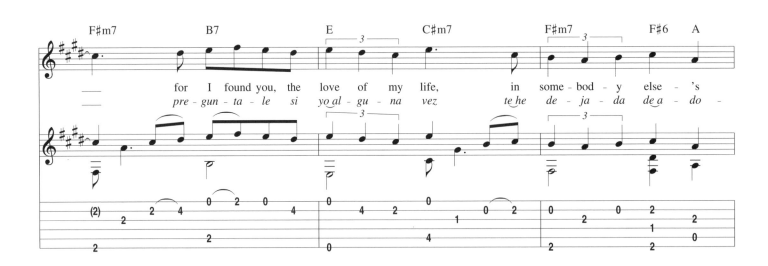

Summer Samba
(So Nice)

Original Words and Music by Marcos Valle and Paulo Sergio Valle
English Words by Norman Gimbel

Drop D Tuning:
① = E ④ = D
② = B ⑤ = A
③ = G ⑥ = D

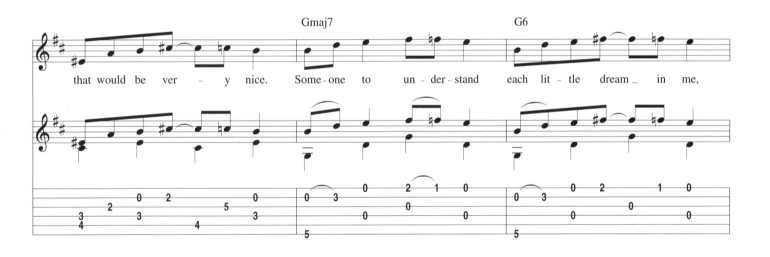

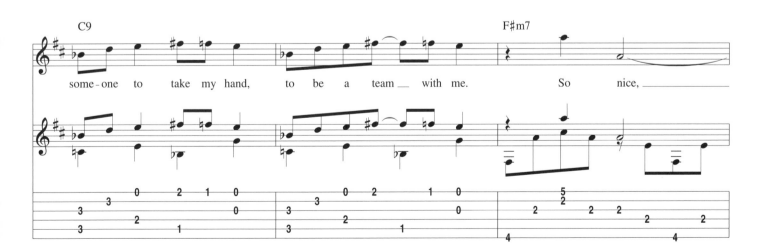

some-one who's read-y to give love a start ___ with me. Oh, yes, ___

___ that would be so nice. ___

Should it be you and me? I could see it would be nice.

nice. ___

Tico Tico
(Tico No Fuba)

Words and Music by Zequinha Abreu, Aloysio Oliveira and Ervin Drake

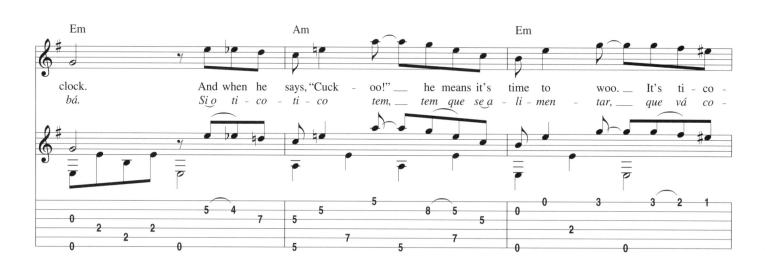

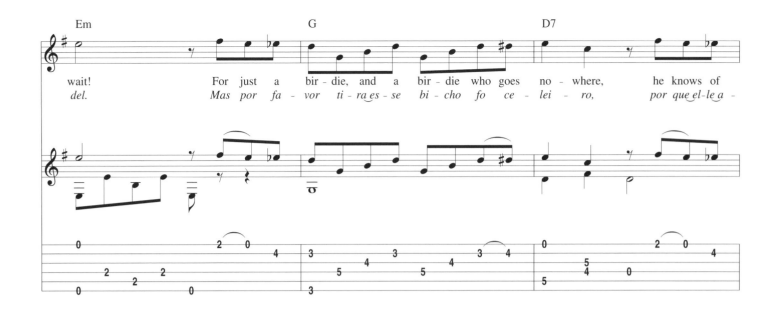

wait! *del.* For just a bir - die, and a bir - die who goes no - where, he knows of
Mas por fa - vor ti - ra es - se bi - cho fo ce - lei - ro, por que el - le a -

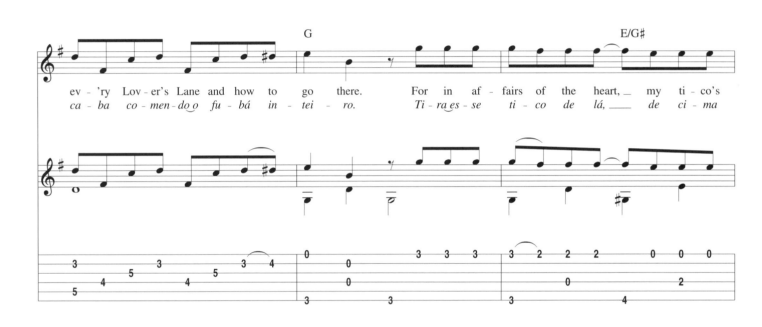

ev - 'ry Lov - er's Lane and how to go there. For in af - fairs of the heart, __ my ti - co's
ca - ba co - men - do o fu - bá in - tei - ro. Ti - ra es - se ti - co de lá, ___ de ci - ma

ter - ri - bly smart, __ he tells me, "Gent - ly, sen - ti - ment - 'ly at the start." Oh, oh, I
do meu fu - bá. ___ Tem tan - ta fru - ta que el - le pu - de pi - ni - car. Eu já fiz

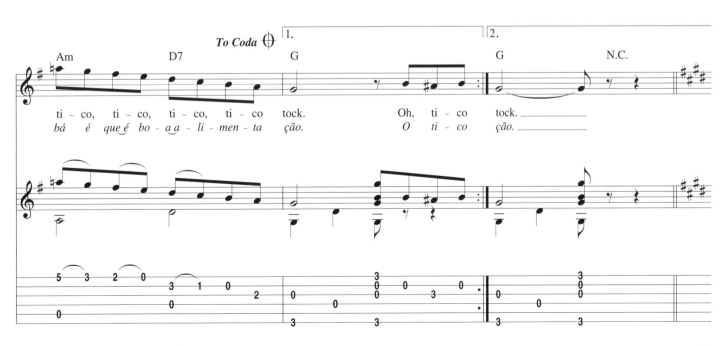

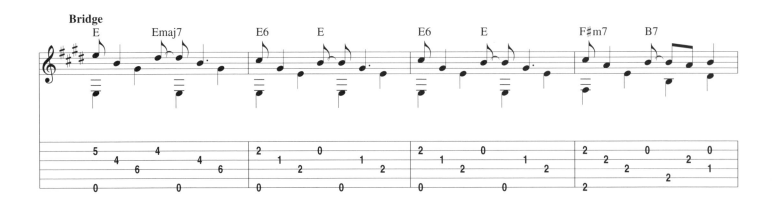

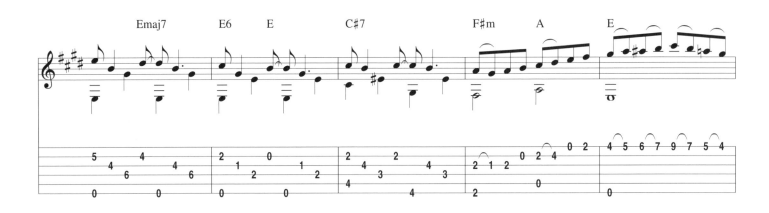

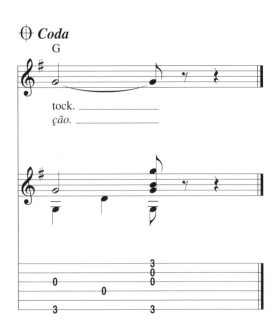

Oh, ti - co,
O ti - co

tock. _____
ção. _____

What a Diff'rence a Day Made

English Words by Stanley Adams
Music and Spanish Words by Maria Grever

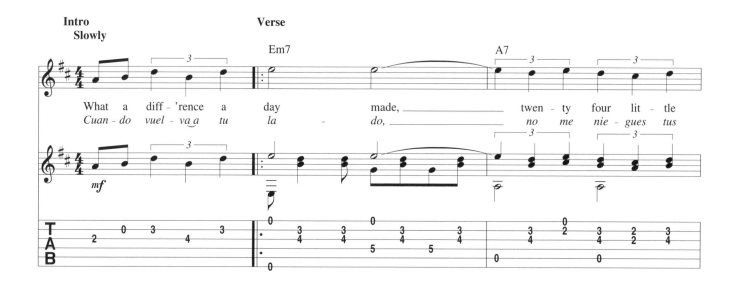

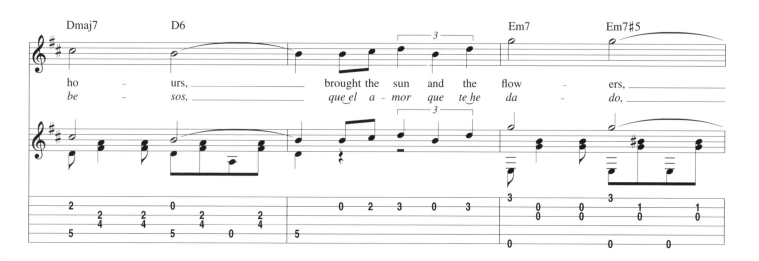

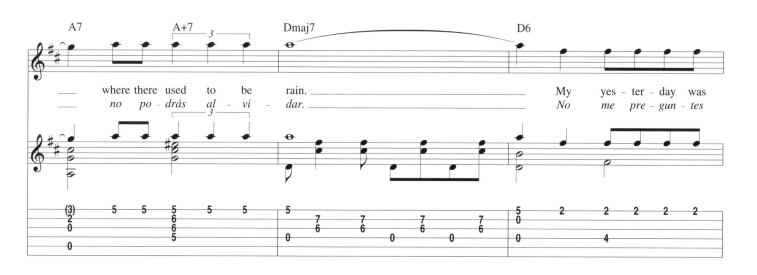

You Belong to My Heart
(Solamente Una Vez)

Music and Spanish Words by Agustin Lara
English Words by Ray Gilbert

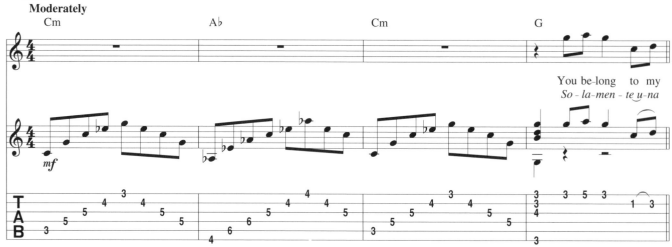

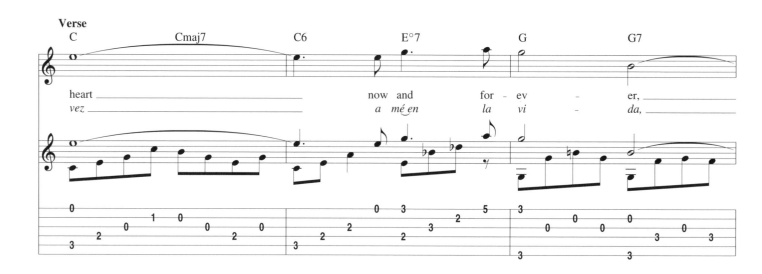

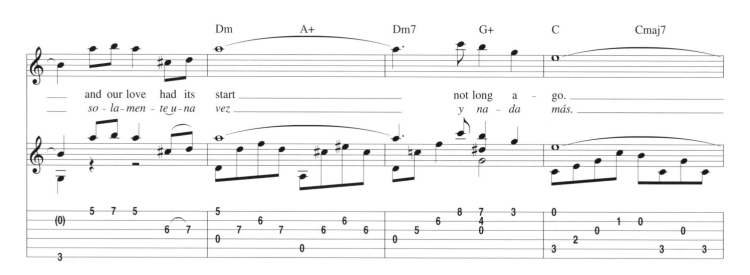

CLASSICAL GUITAR PUBLICATIONS FROM HAL LEONARD

THE BEATLES FOR CLASSICAL GUITAR

Includes 20 solos from big Beatles hits arranged for classical guitar, complete with left-hand and right-hand fingering. Songs include: All My Loving • And I Love Her • Can't Buy Me Love • Fool on the Hill • From a Window • Hey Jude • If I Fell • Let It Be • Michelle • Norwegian Wood • Obla Di • Ticket to Ride • Yesterday • and more. Features arrangements and an introduction by Joe Washington, as well as his helpful hints on classical technique and detailed notes on how to play each song. The book also covers parts and specifications of the classical guitar, tuning, and Joe's "Strata System" – an easy-reading system applied to chord diagrams.

_____00699237 Classical Guitar $16.95

MATTEO CARCASSI – 25 MELODIC AND PROGRESSIVE STUDIES, OP. 60 • *arr. Paul Henry*

One of Carcassi's (1792-1853) most famous collections of classical guitar music – indispensable for the modern guitarist's musical and technical development. Performed by Paul Henry. 49-minute audio accompaniment.

_____00696506 Book/CD Pack $17.95

CLASSICAL & FINGERSTYLE GUITAR TECHNIQUES

by David Oakes • Musicians Institute

This Master Class with MI instructor David Oakes is aimed at any electric or acoustic guitarist who wants a quick, thorough grounding in the essentials of classical and fingerstyle technique. Topics covered include: arpeggios and scales, free stroke and rest stroke, P-i scale technique, three-to-a-string patterns, natural and artificial harmonics, tremolo and rasgueado, and more. The book includes 12 intensive lessons for right and left hand in standard notation & tab, and the CD features 92 solo acoustic tracks.

_____00695171 Book/CD Pack $14.95

CLASSICAL GUITAR CHRISTMAS COLLECTION

Includes classical guitar arrangements in standard notation and tablature for more than two dozen beloved carols: Angels We Have Heard on High • Auld Lang Syne • Ave Maria • Away in a Manger • Canon in D • The First Noel • God Rest Ye Merry, Gentlemen • Hark! the Herald Angels Sing • I Saw Three Ships • Jesu, Joy of Man's Desiring • Joy to the World • O Christmas Tree • O Holy Night • Silent Night • What Child Is This? • and more.

_____00699493 Guitar Solo $9.95

CLASSICAL MASTERPIECES FOR GUITAR

27 works by Bach, Beethoven, Handel, Mendelssohn, Mozart and more transcribed with standard notation and tablature. Now anyone can enjoy classical material regardless of their guitar background. Also features stay-open binding.

_____00699312 ....$12.95

FOR MORE INFORMATION, SEE YOUR LOCAL MUSIC DEALER,
OR WRITE TO:

7777 W. BLUEMOUND RD. P.O. BOX 13819 MILWAUKEE, WI 53213

Visit Hal Leonard Online at **www.halleonard.com**

Prices, contents and availability subject to change without notice.

CLASSICAL THEMES

20 beloved classical themes arranged for easy guitar in large-size notes (with the note names in the note heads) and tablature. Includes: Air on the G String (Bach) • Ave Maria (Schubert) • Für Elise (Beethoven) • In the Hall of the Mountain King (Grieg) • Jesu, Joy of Man's Desiring (Bach) • Largo (Handel) • Ode to Joy (Beethoven) • Pomp and Circumstance (Elgar) • and more. Ideal for beginning or vision-impaired players.

_____00699272 E-Z Play Guitar $8.95

MASTERWORKS FOR GUITAR

Over 60 Favorites from Four Centuries • World's Great Classical Music

Dozens of classical masterpieces: Allemande • Bourree • Canon in D • Jesu, Joy of Man's Desiring • Lagrima • Malaguena • Mazurka • Piano Sonata No. 14 in C# Minor (Moonlight) Op. 27 No. 2 First Movement Theme • Ode to Joy • Prelude No. I (Well-Tempered Clavier).

_____00699503 ....$16.95

A MODERN APPROACH TO CLASSICAL GUITAR • *by Charles Duncan*

This multi-volume method was developed to allow students to study the art of classical guitar within a new, more contemporary framework. For private, class or self-instruction. Book One incorporates chord frames and symbols, as well as a recording to assist in tuning and to provide accompaniments for at-home practice. Book One also introduces beginning fingerboard technique and music theory. Book Two and Three build upon the techniques learned in Book One.

_____00695114 Book 1 – Book Only..$6.95
_____00695113 Book 1 – Book/CD Pack..$10.95
_____00695116 Book 2 – Book Only..$6.95
_____00695115 Book 2 – Book/CD Pack..$10.95
_____00699202 Book 3 – Book Only..$7.95
_____00695117 Book 3 – Book/CD Pack..$10.95
_____00695119 Composite Book/CD Pack..$24.95

ANDRES SEGOVIA – 20 STUDIES FOR GUITAR • *Sor/Segovia*

20 studies for the classical guitar written by Beethoven's contemporary, Fernando Sor, revised, edited and fingered by the great classical guitarist Andres Segovia. These essential repertoire pieces continue to be used by teachers and students to build solid classical technique. Features a 50-minute demonstration CD.

_____00695012 Book/CD Pack $17.95
_____00006363 Book Only..$6.95

THE FRANCISCO TÁRREGA COLLECTION

edited and performed by Paul Henry

Considered the father of modern classical guitar, Francisco Tárrega revolutionized guitar technique and composed a wealth of music that will be a cornerstone of classical guitar repertoire for centuries to come. This unique book/CD pack features 14 of his most outstanding pieces in standard notation and tab, edited and performed on CD by virtuoso Paul Henry. Includes: Adelita • Capricho Árabe • Estudio Brillante • Grand Jota • Lágrima • Malagueña • María • Recuerdos de la Alhambra • Tango • and more, plus bios of Tárrega and Henry.

_____00698993 Book/CD Pack $17.95

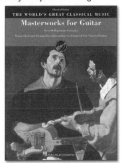

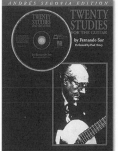

1202